BIG NOTE

BEATLES' B

Arranged by SHANNON M. GRAMA

HAL•LEONARD®
CORPORATION

7777 W. BLUEMOUND RD. P.O. BOX 13819 MILWAUKEE, WI 53213

BIG NOTE

BEATLES' BEST

CONTENTS

ALL MY LOVING

Words and Music by
JOHN LENNON and PAUL McCARTNEY

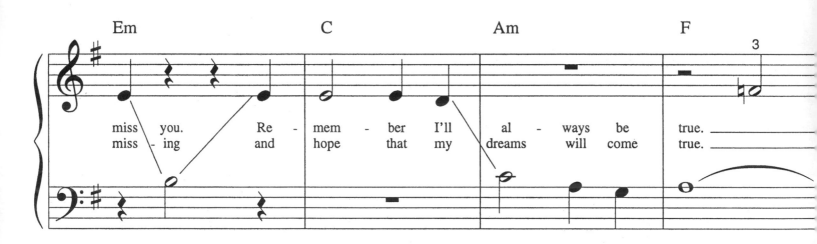

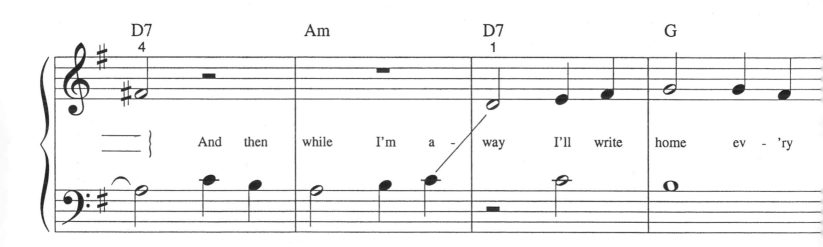

AND I LOVE HER

Words and Music by
JOHN LENNON and PAUL McCARTNEY

MCA music publishing

CAN'T BUY ME LOVE

Words and Music by
JOHN LENNON and PAUL McCARTNEY

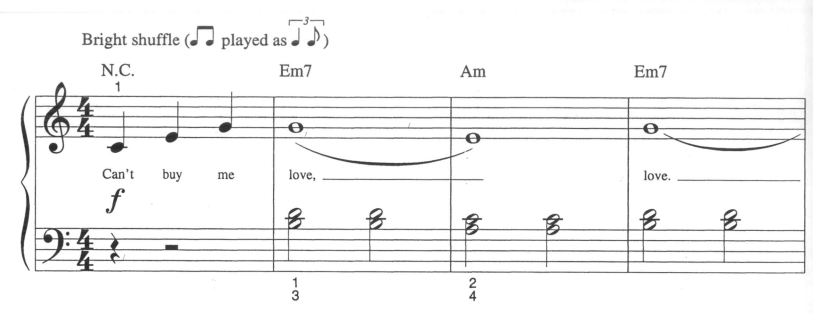

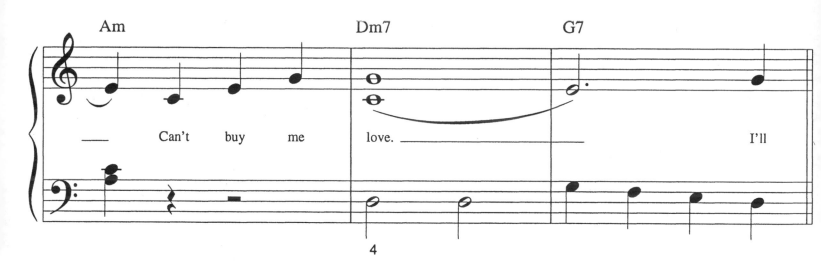

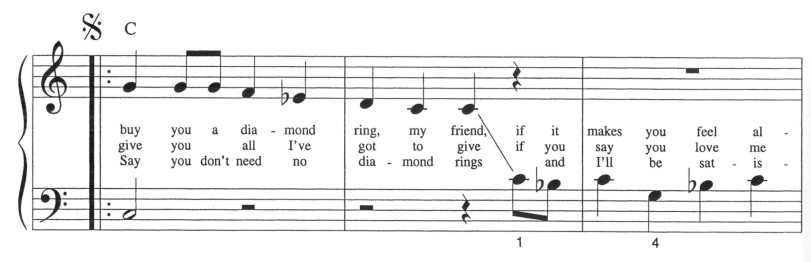

DAY TRIPPER

Words and Music by
JOHN LENNON and PAUL McCARTNEY

MCA music publishing

12

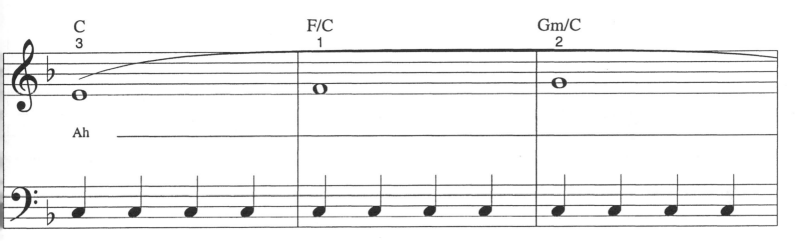

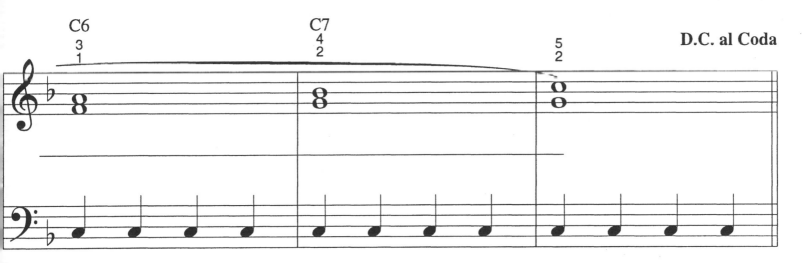

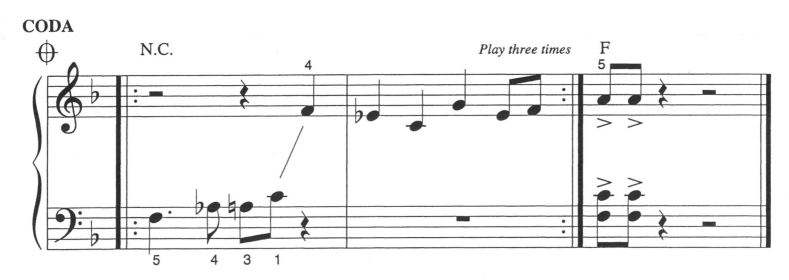

EIGHT DAYS A WEEK

Words and Music by
JOHN LENNON and PAUL McCARTNEY

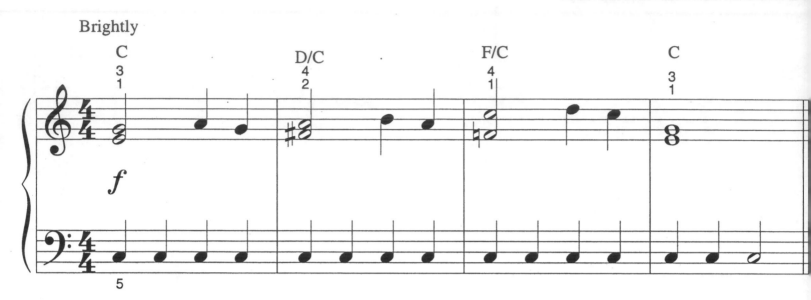

Ooh, I need your love, babe. Guess you know it's true.
Love you ev-'ry day, babe girl. Al-ways on my mind.

Hope you need my love, babe, just like I need you.
One thing I can say, babe, girl, love you all the time.

ELEANOR RIGBY

Words and Music by
JOHN LENNON and PAUL McCARTNEY

THE FOOL ON THE HILL

Words and Music by
JOHN LENNON and PAUL McCARTNEY

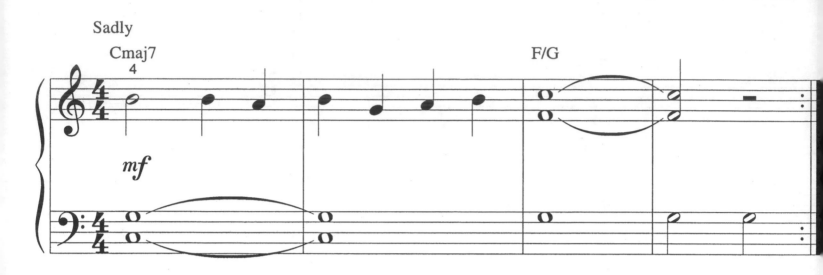

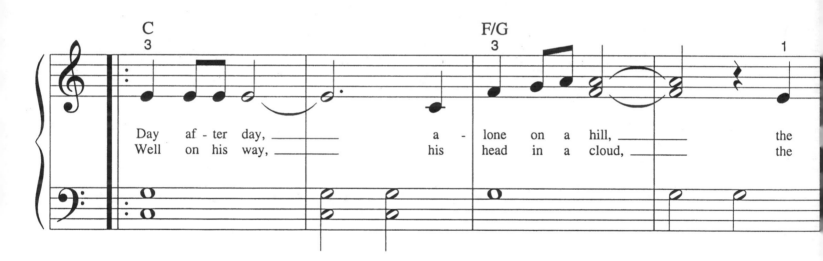

Day af-ter day, _____ a-lone on a hill, _____ the
Well on his way, _____ his head in a cloud, _____ the

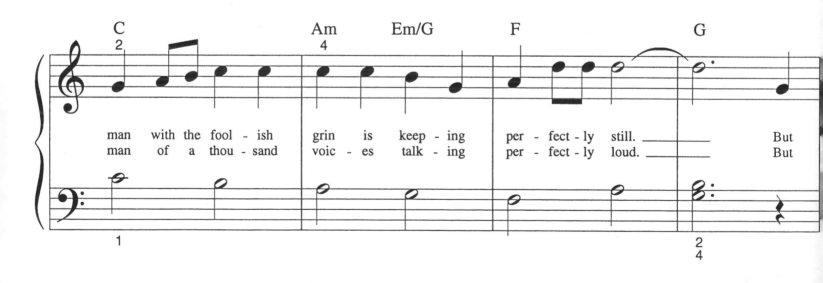

man with the fool-ish grin is keep-ing per-fect-ly still. _____ But
man of a thou-sand voic-es talk-ing per-fect-ly loud. _____ But

world _____ spin - ing 'round.

GOOD DAY SUNSHINE

Words and Music by
JOHN LENNON and PAUL McCARTNEY

With a steady beat (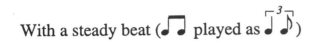)

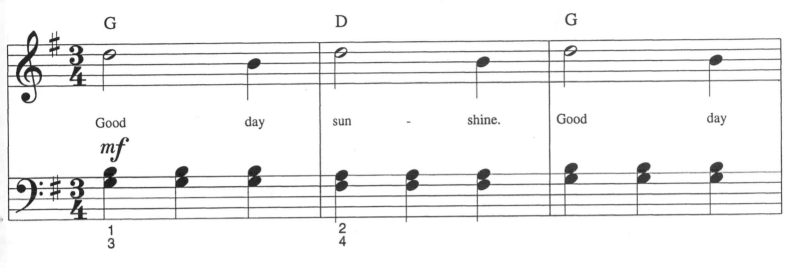

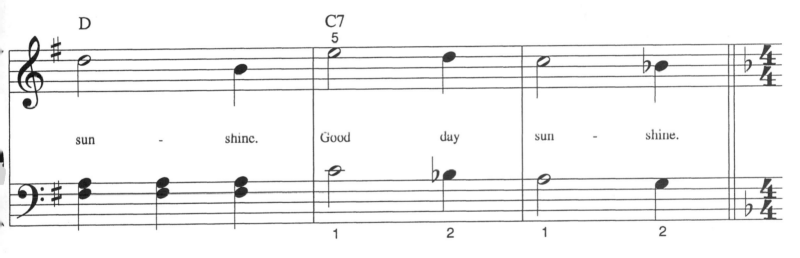

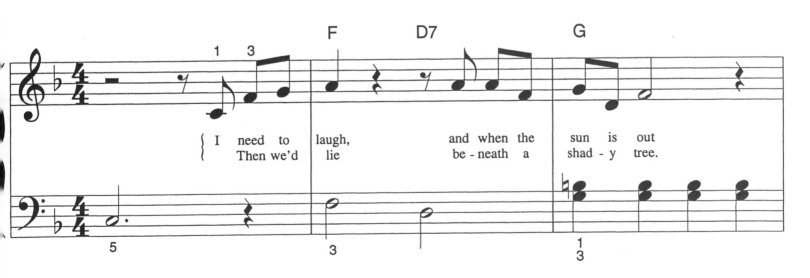

24

We take a walk. The sun is shin-ing down.

Burns my feet as they touch the ground. _____

D.C. al Coda

CODA

Good day sun-shine. Good day sun-shine. _____

GET BACK

Words and Music by
JOHN LENNON and PAUL McCARTNEY

MCA music publishing

A HARD DAY'S NIGHT

Words and Music by
JOHN LENNON and PAUL McCARTNEY

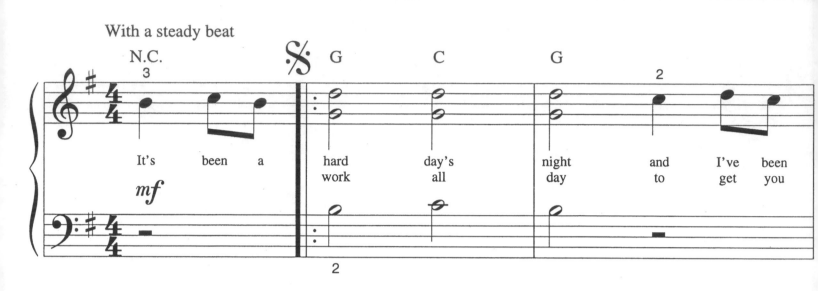

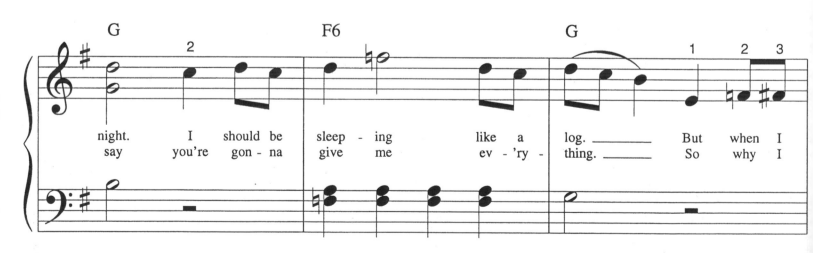

MCA music publishing

To Coda

HELP!

Words and Music by
JOHN LENNON and PAUL McCARTNEY

Moderately, with a driving beat

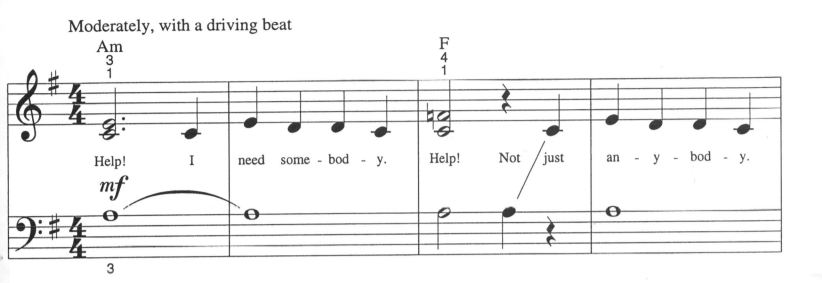

Help! I need some-bod-y. Help! Not just an-y-bod-y.

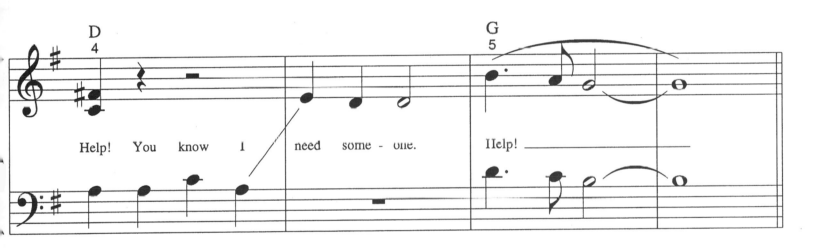

Help! You know I need some-one. Help!

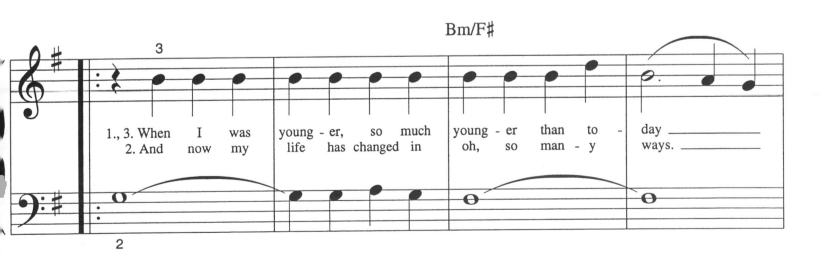

1., 3. When I was young-er, so much young-er than to-day
2. And now my life has changed in oh, so man-y ways.

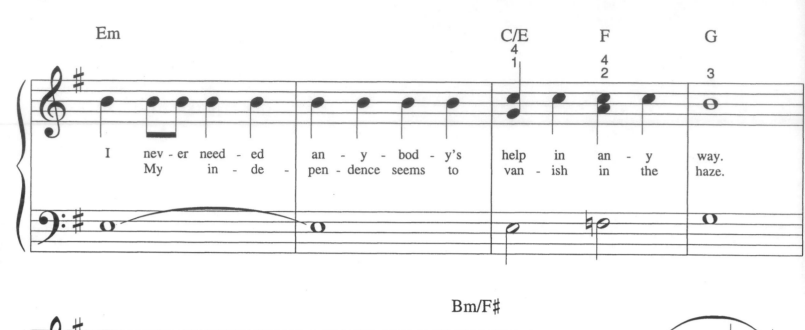

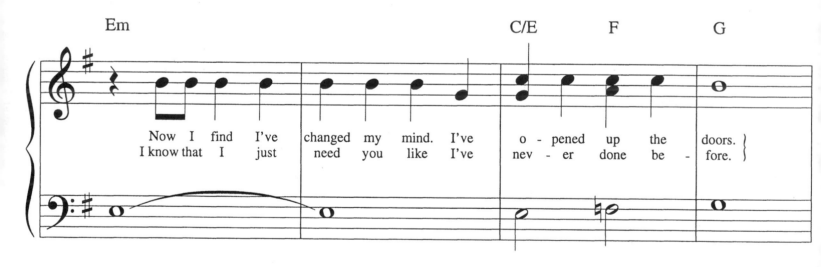

HERE, THERE AND EVERYWHERE

Words and Music by
JOHN LENNON and PAUL McCARTNEY

Freely

To lead a bet-ter life   I need my love to be   here.

Slowly, with a beat

Here,
There,

mak - ing   each   day   of   the
run - ning   my   hands   through   her

year,
hair,

chang - ing   my   life   with   a
both   of   us   think - ing   how

HEY JUDE

Words and Music by
JOHN LENNON and PAUL McCARTNEY

LET IT BE

Words and Music by
JOHN LENNON and PAUL McCARTNEY

THE LONG AND WINDING ROAD

Words and Music by
JOHN LENNON and PAUL McCARTNEY

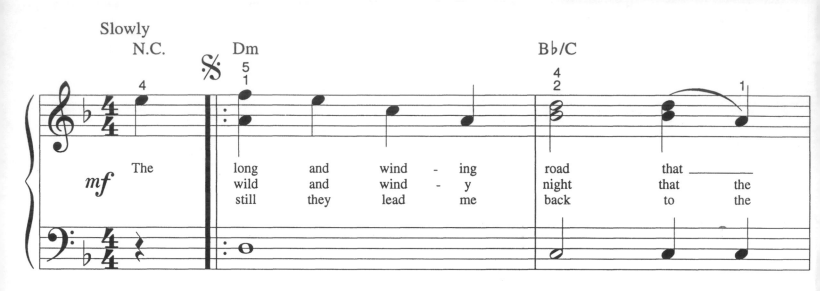

MCA music publishing

43

MICHELLE

Words and Music by
JOHN LENNON and PAUL McCARTNEY

Moderate tempo

MCA music publishing

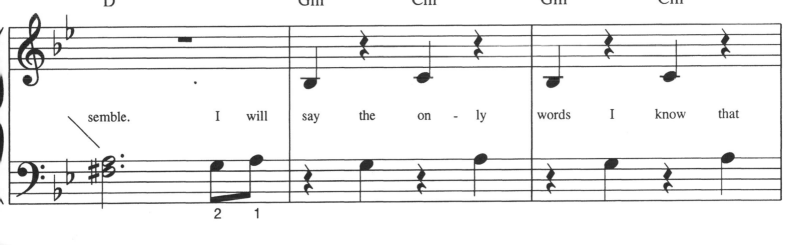

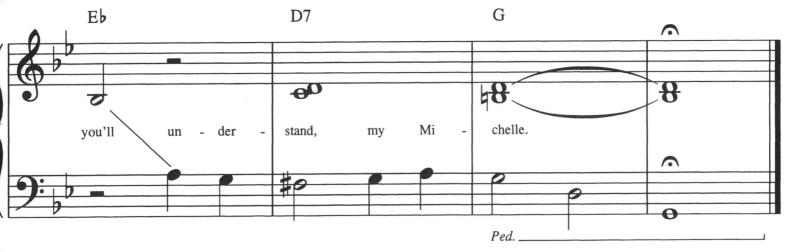

I WANT TO HOLD YOUR HAND

Words and Music by
JOHN LENNON and PAUL McCARTNEY

NORWEGIAN WOOD
(This Bird Has Flown)

Words and Music by
JOHN LENNON and PAUL McCARTNEY

52

NOWHERE MAN

Words and Music by
JOHN LENNON and PAUL McCARTNEY

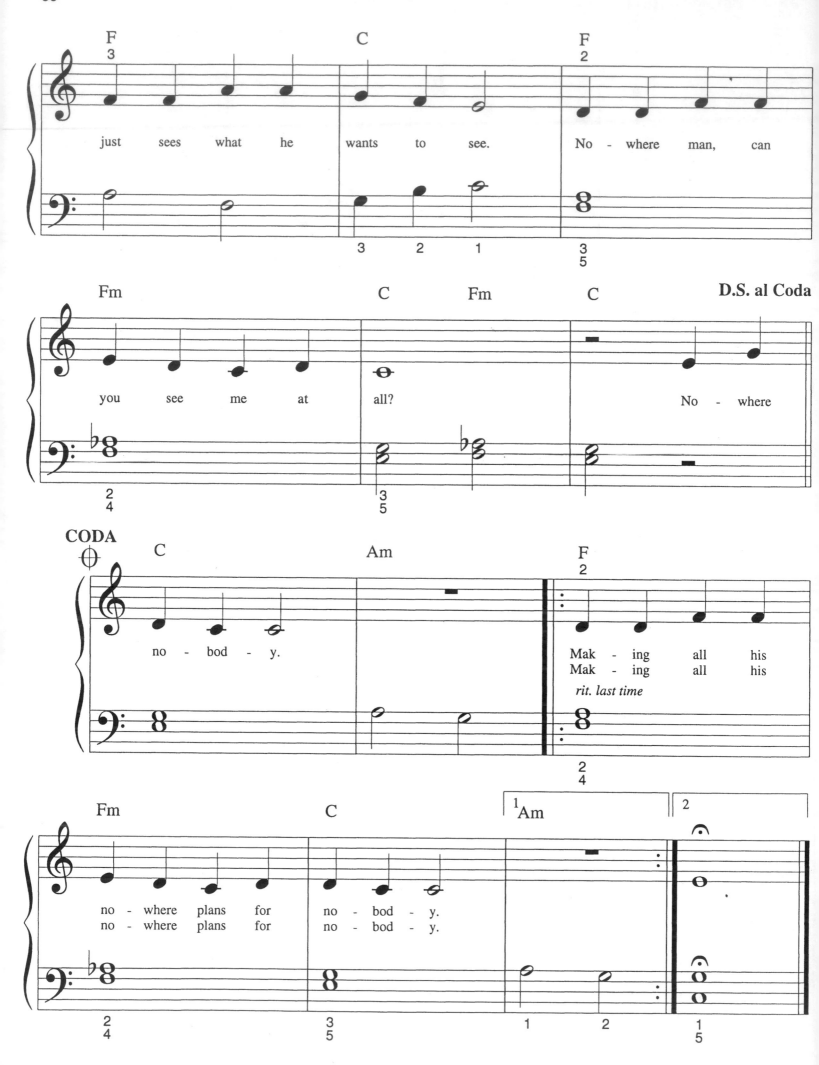

WE CAN WORK IT OUT

Words and Music by
JOHN LENNON and PAUL McCARTNEY

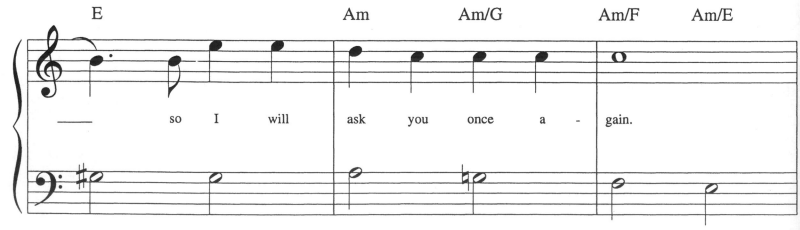

OB-LA-DI, OB-LA-DA

Words and Music by
JOHN LENNON and PAUL McCARTNEY

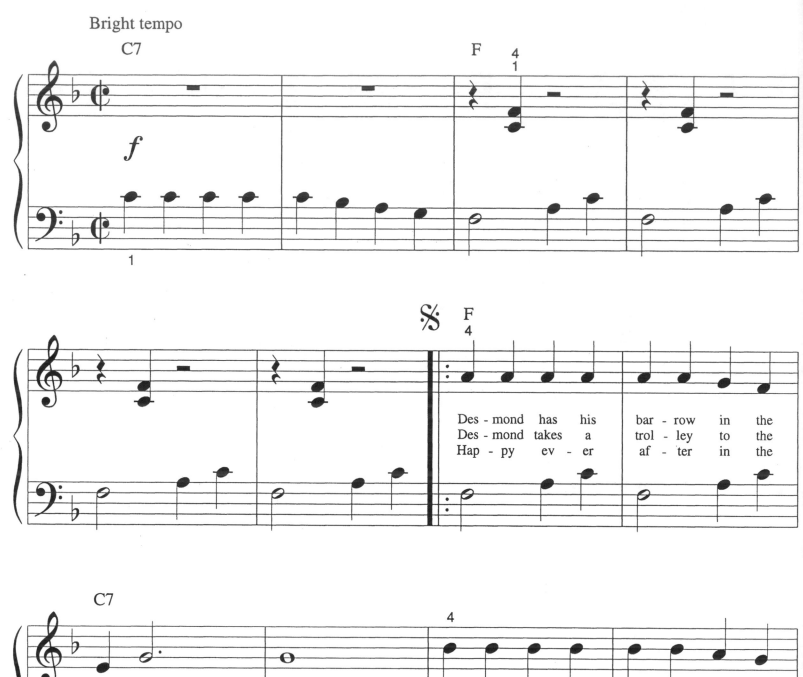

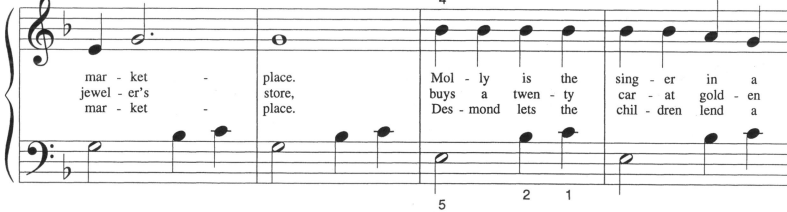

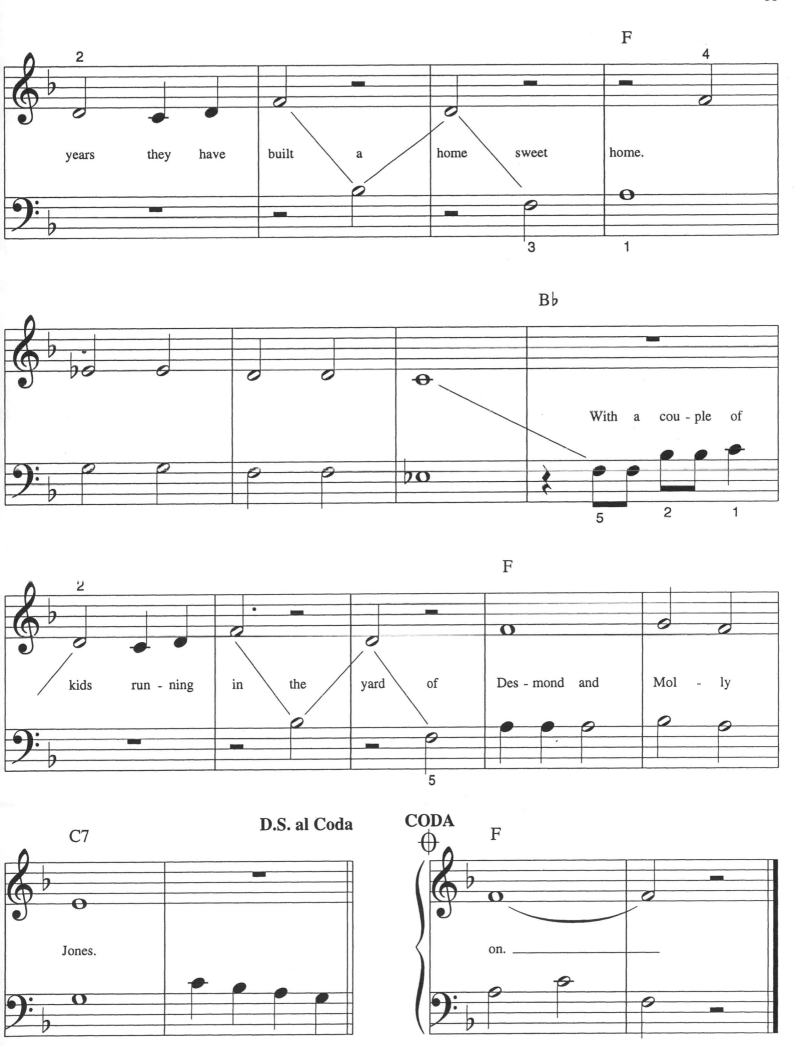

SOMETHING

By GEORGE HARRISON

Gently

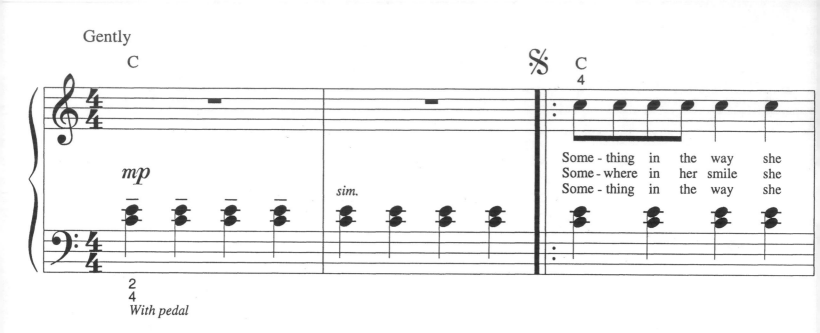

With pedal

TICKET TO RIDE

Words and Music by
JOHN LENNON and PAUL McCARTNEY

Moderate rock tempo

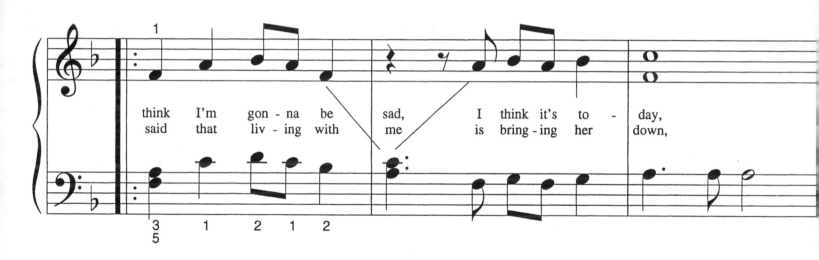

think I'm gon-na be sad, I think it's to-day,
said that liv-ing with me is bring-ing her down,

yeah. The girl that's driv-ing me mad is go-ing a-
yeah. For she would nev-er be free when I was a-

MCA music publishing

high, _____ she ought to think twice, ought to do right by me. Be -

Bb

fore she gets to say - in' good - bye _____ she ought to think twice, ought to do right by

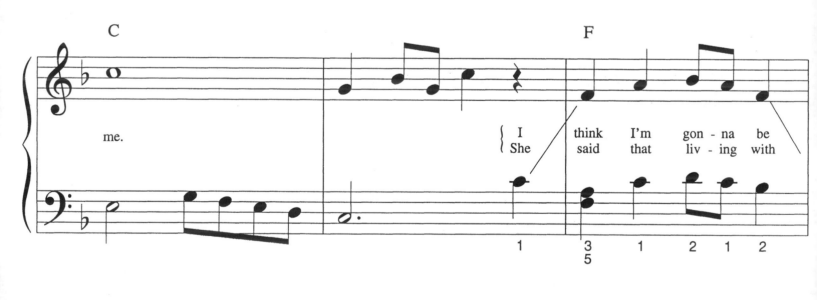

C   F

me.   I   think I'm   gon - na   be
                                 She   said   that liv - ing with

1   3   1   2   1   2
    5

                                                                    3

sad,   I think it's to - day,   yeah.   The
me   is bring - ing her down,   yeah.   For

WHEN I'M SIXTY-FOUR

Words and Music by
JOHN LENNON and PAUL McCARTNEY

WITH A LITTLE HELP
FROM MY FRIENDS

Words and Music by
JOHN LENNON and PAUL McCARTNEY

MCA music publishing

YESTERDAY

Words and Music by
JOHN LENNON and PAUL McCARTNEY

MCA music publishing

YELLOW SUBMARINE

Words and Music by
JOHN LENNON and PAUL McCARTNEY

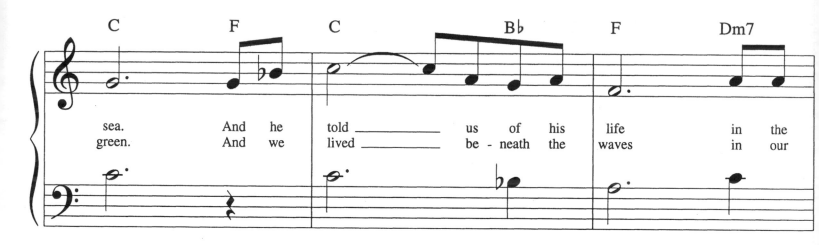

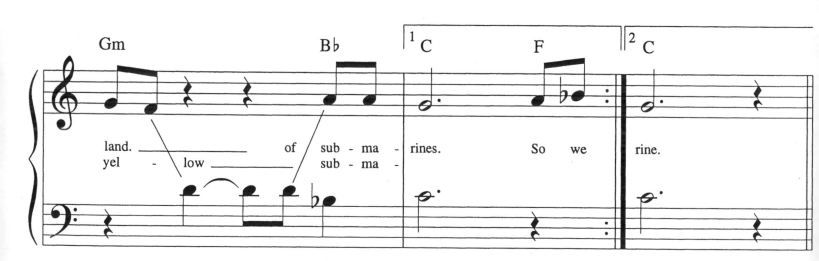